The Effects of Prayer in the Life of a Leader

A 12-Month Leadership Training Workbook

By

Dr. Valarie Williams Harris

The Effects of Prayer in the Life of a Leader

Published by:
Stepping Out With Purpose, LLC
www.talktimeval.com

Book Creation and Design
GermanCreative
Interior Design
Valarie W. Harris

ISBN for hardcover version: 979-8-88862-490-6
ISBN for eBook version: 979-8-88862-777-8

Printed in the United States of America

Dedication

Dedicated to all leaders who allow God
to be the source of their leadership role
in the Body of Christ. You have greatness
inside of you that others need to be successful.
You are ambassadors uniquely chosen
to do great things in the world.

"The Lord makes firm the steps of the one
who delights in him."
Psalm 37:23

INTRODUCTION

As a servant leader, it is essential to understand your mandate and responsibility to lead others in the right direction and show them what it means to serve first. Leadership development is necessary if you want your team to be successful. It is essential to have a clear vision and attainable goals. It is vital to provide your organization with information, knowledge, and different methods to achieve those goals so you can move to a higher level in ministry. There are so many different approaches that can help you lead a group of individuals who are motivated and excited about reaching beyond their starting point as a leader.

Throughout this training workbook experience, you will explore various ways to approach leadership teams. The workbook shares helpful information for training purposes that will help leaders reach the next level. We must ask ourselves, Are you ready to fulfill God's plan for your life? Are you prepared to be obedient to follow God's instructions when leading? Being a leader has its ups and downs. You can't give up or quit when something doesn't go your way. You have to persevere and ask God to show you what to do and how you need to go forth. You might fall, but you can and will get back up.

The workbook includes various activities such as biblical leadership examples, leader characteristics, leadership principles, personal evaluations, qualities of a leader, icebreaker games, competencies, spiritual gifts surveys, communication assessments, leadership styles, and personality tests. Personally and professionally, I have examined some of the material in this workbook. The journaling challenge included in the workbook will help leaders to simplify the information, making it more user-friendly for leaders to use with their teams. Merriam-Webster Dictionary defines leadership as the office or position of a leader or the capacity to lead. John Maxwell defines leadership this way: "Leadership is the ability and act of guiding and motivating a group of people toward a common goal."

The shared strategies will help leadership teams build stronger bonds as they work together. The slogan "TEAMWORK MAKES THE DREAM WORK" has demonstrated its authenticity. According to Ecclesiastes 4:9-10 "Two are better than one because they have a good reward for their labor. For if they fall, one will lift his companion. But woe to him who is alone when he falls, For he has no one to help him up." (NKJV)

THE EFFECTIVENESS OF PRAYER FOR LEADERS

This leadership training workbook will serve as a resource for Christian leaders to follow as they model a lifestyle of prayer. Leadership and devotion to prayer go hand in hand and are necessary if you want your team to succeed. The importance of prayer brings about an act of obedience and the solution to the situation or problems one might encounter. Jesus taught this when He got up before daybreak and went to a solitary place to pray Mark 1:35.

- UNDERSTANDING PRAYER
- THE PURPOSE OF PRAYER
- HOW TO PRATICE A LIFESTYLE OF PRAYER
- BUILDING RELATIONSHIPS
- SETTING ASIDE TIME
- TIME-MANAGEMENT
- PRIORITIZING YOUR TIME
- UNDERSTANDING THE BIBLICAL PERSPECTIVE OF LEADERSHIP
- WHAT IS LEADERSHIP
- LEADERSHIP QUALITIES
- LEADERSHIP STYLES
- SERVANT LEADERSHIP
- ICEBREAKERS/GAME ACTIVITIES

UNDERSTANDING PRAYER

Define Prayer

The Merriam-Webster dictionary defines prayer this way: "An address such as a petition to God or a god in word or thought" (Merriam-Webster Dictionary, 2021). The Lexicon dictionary defines prayer as a solemn request for help or expression of thanks addressed to God or an object of worship (Lexicon, 2021). In Hebrew, several words are translated to mean prayer. Three translations are defined in this manual including tephillah (H8605), palal (H6419), and siah (H7879).

The Bible presents various biblical meanings of prayer showing how individuals talked, praised, and made their requests known to God. Many scriptures illustrated times where people cried out to God asking Him for protection, guidance, strength, healing, mercy, forgiveness, and deliverance. Romans 12:12 states, "Rejoice in hope, be patient in tribulations, be constant in prayer (Bible E. S., 2008)."

METHODS OF PRAYER

- The Lord's Prayer
- ACTS Prayer
- Corporate Prayer
- Prayer Walking
- Prayer Journaling
- Praying the Scripture

TYPES OF PRAYER

- The Prayer of Faith
- Prayer of Agreement
- Prayer of the Holy Spirit
- Prayer of Intercession
- Prayer of Petition
- The Prayer of Thanksgiving
- Prayer of Worship

THE IMPORTANCE OF PRAYER

The importance of prayer brings about an act of obedience and the solution to the situation or problems one might encounter. Jesus taught this when He got up before daybreak and went to a lonely place to pray Mark 1:35. Prayer allows time to make requests on behalf of oneself and others.

FOR MORE INFORMATION

CONTACT
DR. VALARIE WILLIAMS HARRIS
https://linktr.ee/talktimeval

JANUARY

NAME THREE METHODS OF PRAYER.

____
○ _____________________________
○ _____________________________
○ _____________________________

NAME THREE TYPES OF PRAYER
____

____

____

WORD FOR THE MONTH: PRAYER
____

____

____

DATE
____

VISION STATEMENT

MISSION STATEMENT
____

____

YEARLY GOALS
○ _____________________________
○ _____________________________
○ _____________________________

HOW WOULD YOU RANK TODAY'S MEETING?

☆ ☆ ☆ ☆ ☆

5 Minute Prayer Journaling

"FOR I KNOW THE PLANS I HAVE FOR YOU" DECLARES THE LORD
"PLANS TO PROSPER YOU AND NOT TO HARM YOU. PLANS TO
GIVE YOU HOPE AND A FUTURE"

Jeremiah 29:11

Jesus' Prayer Practices

Prayer is a powerful tool to practice if you want to be a healthy leader. Jesus shows us that the practice of prayer is essential. The Old and New Testaments speak that prayer can empower us to be better people.

The Prayer Practice of Jesus

Fill in the blanks with the correct answer using the scriptures given.

1. "And after he had dismissed the crowds, He went up on the ______________ by himself to pray." (Matthew 14:23)

2. "Then Jesus went with them to a place called ____________, and he said to his disciples, "Sit here, while I go over there and pray." (Matthew 26:36)

3. "And rising very early in the morning, while it was still dark, he departed and went out to a __________, and there he prayed." (Mark 1:35)

4. "But he would ____________ to desolate places and pray." (Luke 5:16)

5. "In these days he went out to the mountain to pray, and ___ ______ he continued in prayer to God." (Luke 6:12)

6. "And he told them a parable to the effect that they ought always to _______ and not lose heart." (Luke 18:1)

7. "if my _______ who are called by my name humble themselves and _____ and seek my face and turn from their wicked ways, then I will hear from heaven and will forgive their sin and heal their land." (2 Chronicles 7:14)

8. Isaiah points out the need for us to pray when writing the following words, "He gives power to the faint, and to him who has no might he increases strength. Even youths shall faint and be weary, and young men shall fall exhausted, but they who wait for the Lord shall renew their strength; they shall mount up with wings like eagles; they shall run and not be weary; they shall walk and not faint." (Isaiah 40:29-31)

JESUS TAUGHT US HOW TO PRAY

All leaders must understand the power of words. Proverbs 18:21 says, "Death and life are in the power of the tongue." As a leader, you can positively or negatively affect those you lead. Be the leader that leads with love and compassion as you build others up. The way to stay in tune with God is through prayer, especially when making decisions with the words you use towards others. The disciple observed the prayer life of Jesus, and they wanted to know how to pray. "Now Jesus was praying in a certain place, and when he finished, one of his disciples said to him, "Lord, teach us to pray, as John taught his disciples." And he said to them, "When you pray, say:

"Father, hallowed be your name.
Your kingdom come.
Give us each day our daily bread,
and forgive us our sins,
for we ourselves forgive everyone who is indebted to us.
And lead us not into temptation." Luke 11:1-4

Why Should We Pray

- According to (Ephesians 6:18-19; Philippians 4:6-7; These: 5:15-18) We are commanded to pray.
- Prayer brings our request to God. (Matthew 7:7, 1 John 5:14-15)
- Prayer helps to discern the will of God. (Isaiah 30:21)
- Prayer helps us overcome struggles in our lives. (Matthew 26:41; Luke 6:12-13)
- Prayer causes us to glorify God. (Luke 2:36-38; 1 Thessalonians 5:18)

Match the following verses with the correct scripture.

1. "Do not be anxious about anything, but in everything by prayer and supplication with thanksgiving let your requests be made known to God."
2. "Watch and pray that you may not enter into temptation. The spirit indeed is willing, but the flesh is weak."
3. "Give thanks in all circumstances; for this is the will of God in Christ Jesus for you."
4. "And your ears shall hear a word behind you, saying, "This is the way, walk in it," when you turn to the right or when you turn to the left."
5. "Ask, and it will be given to you; seek, and you will find; knock, and it will be opened to you."

Name: ________________   **Date:** _____________

Weekly Prayer Practice

Activity	S	M	T	W	T	F	S
Morning Prayer							
Bible Study							
Prayer Partner							
Memorizing Scripture							
Prayer Journaling							
Writing a Love Letter to Jesus							
Listening to Bible Audio							
Recording Verses you Memorize							
Post-Weekly Scriptures							
Reading Scriptures							

Morning Checklist

Top 10 Prayer Priorities

- GOD
- FAMILY
- WORK
- MINISTRY
- HEALTH
- LIVING ENVIRONMENT
- FINANCES
- COMMUNITY
- SPIRITUAL GROWTH
- GROWTH MINDSET

MY NOTES

THE PURPOSE OF PRAYER

The purpose of prayer is to glorify God by giving adoration, thanksgiving, repentance, and petition. Prayer will build your faith and is the armor you need to defeat the attack of the enemy. Prayer is how we join in partnership with God. The Collins Harper Dictionary (2021) defines a partnership as a relationship in which two or more people, organizations, or countries work together as partners. When one has a partnership with God, it will allow them to communicate with one another. Communication is an act, an instance of speaking, the imparting or exchanging information, ideas, or feelings (Harper, 2021).

It happens when a person has open communication with God. An exchange takes place. As this communication exchange takes place, it opens the conversation so a person's request can be made known to God. It is a way to build trust in God, showing one's dependence on Him in all situations. Relying on God shows Him how much a person needs Him.

What is the purpose of prayer?

____
____
____
____
____

February

MEETING GOALS

○ _______________________
○ _______________________
○ _______________________

LIST THE THINGS THAT
COMMUNICATION IS AN ACT OF:

○ _______________________
○ _______________________
○ _______________________
○ _______________________

WORD FOR THE MONTH:
COMMUNICATION

WAYS YOU PLAN ON PROMOTING
COMMUNICATION WITH TEAM
MEMBERS.

WHEN ONE HAS A PARTNERSHIP
WITH GOD WHAT DOES IT ALLOW?

WHAT HAPPENS WHEN A PERSON
HAS AN OPEN COMMUNICATION
WITH GOD?

HOW WOULD YOU RANK TODAY'S
MEETING?

☆ ☆ ☆ ☆ ☆

5 Minute Prayer Journaling

"Rejoice always, pray without ceasing, give thanks in all circumstances; for this is the will of God in Christ Jesus for you"
1 Thessalonians 5:16-18

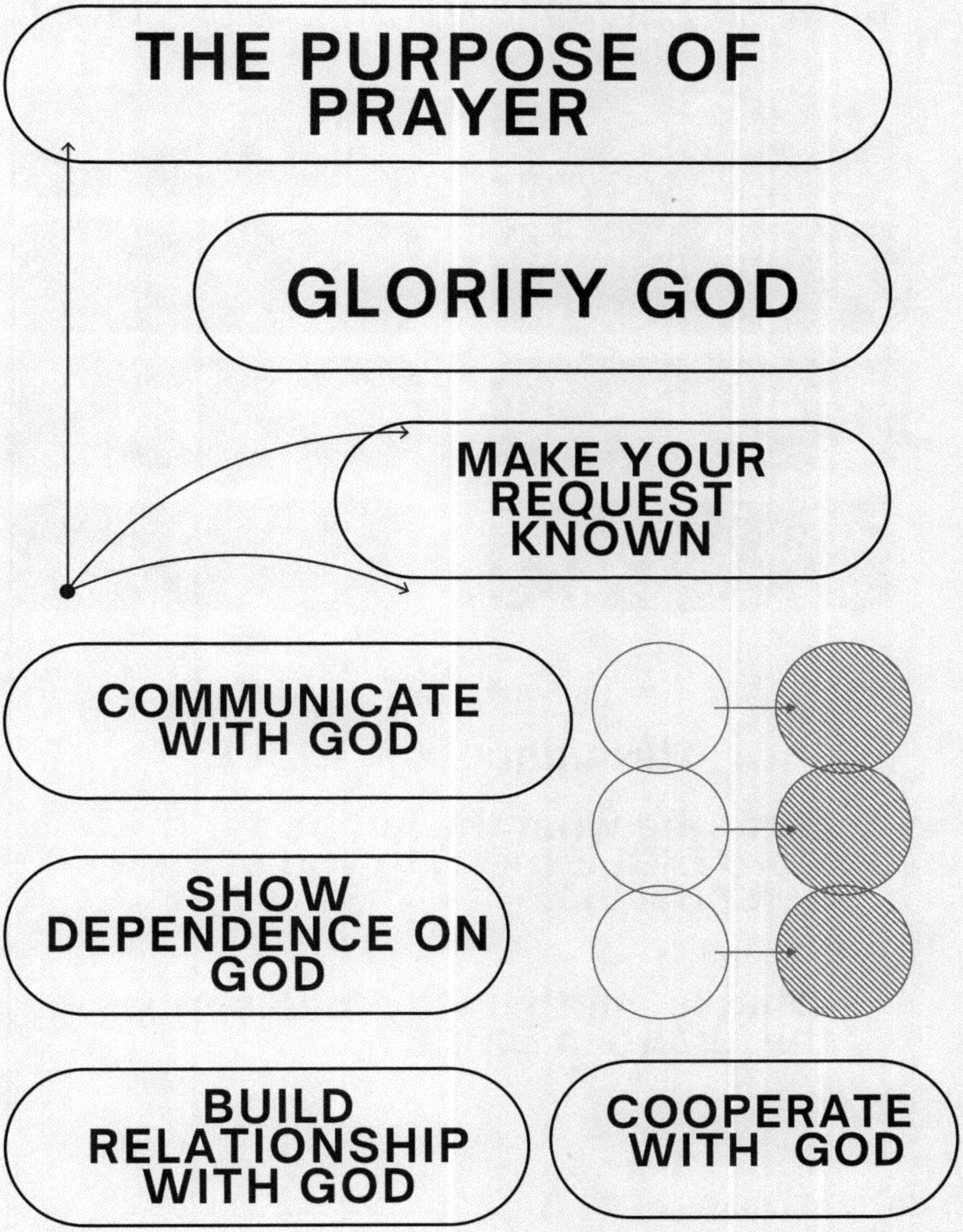

THE PURPOSE OF PRAYER

GLORIFY GOD

MAKE YOUR REQUEST KNOWN

COMMUNICATE WITH GOD

SHOW DEPENDENCE ON GOD

BUILD RELATIONSHIP WITH GOD

COOPERATE WITH GOD

WAYS TO COMMUNICATE WITH GOD

VERBAL	Praying throughout the day
VISUAL	Scripture Reading
LISTENING	Hearing the Scripture on Audio
WRITTEN	Listening in Silence

How God Speaks

Throughout the BIBLE

Describe what the letters for the word BIBLE mean to you in your personal life.

What is another way to describe the letters in BIBLE?

B _______________________

I _______________________

B _______________________

L _______________________

E _______________________

Living on Purpose

LEADERS WHO PRAYED IN THE BIBLE

Daniel and David Prayed three times a day

They both knew the importance of prayer.

Daniel Prayed
Daniel 6:10

NOW WHEN DANIEL KNEW THAT THE WRITING WAS SIGNED, HE WENT HOME. AND IN HIS UPPER ROOM, WITH HIS WINDOWS OPEN TOWARD JERUSALEM, HE KNELT DOWN ON HIS KNEES THREE TIMES THAT DAY, AND PRAYED AND GAVE THANKS BEFORE HIS GOD, AS WAS HIS CUSTOM SINCE EARLY DAYS.

David Prayed
David 55:15-16

AS FOR ME, I WILL CALL UPON GOD, AND THE LORD SHALL SAVE ME. EVENING AND MORNING AND AT NOON I WILL PRAY, AND CRY ALOUD, AND HE SHALL HEAR MY VOICE.

Joshua Prayed
Joshua 10:12-13

ON THE DAY THE LORD GAVE THE ISRAELITES VICTORY OVER THE AMORITES, JOSHUA PRAYED TO THE LORD IN FRONT OF ALL THE PEOPLE OF ISRAEL. HE SAID, "LET THE SUN STAND STILL OVER GIBEON, AND THE MOON OVER THE VALLEY OF AIJALON." SO THE SUN STOOD STILL AND THE MOON STAYED IN PLACE UNTIL THE NATION OF ISRAEL HAD DEFEATED ITS ENEMIES. — JOSHUA

Jeremiah Prayed
Jeremiah 33:3

"CALL TO ME AND I WILL ANSWER YOU AND TELL YOU GREAT AND UNSEARCHABLE THINGS YOU DO NOT KNOW."

Deborah Prayed
Judges 5:6-7, 12

"In the days of Shamgar son of Anath, in the days of Jael, the highways were abandoned; travelers took to winding paths. Villagers in Israel would not fight; they held back until I, Deborah, arose, until I arose, a mother in Israel. ... 'Wake up, wake up, Deborah! Wake up, wake up, break out in song! Arise, Barak! Take captive your captives, son of Abinoam.'"

Abraham Prayed
Genesis 20:17

THEN ABRAHAM PRAYED TO GOD; AND GOD HEALED ABIMELECH, AND ALSO HEALED HIS WIFE AND FEMALE SLAVES SO THAT THEY BORE CHILDREN.

Nehemiah Prayed
Nehemiah 1:5

AND I SAID, "O LORD GOD OF HEAVEN, THE GREAT AND AWESOME GOD WHO KEEPS COVENANT AND STEADFAST LOVE WITH THOSE WHO LOVE HIM AND KEEP HIS COMMANDMENTS.

God hears and answers prayers

Activity Sheet

Use the previous page to answer the following questions

What happened after Abram prayed for Abimelech?

⊙   ____

⊙   ____

⊙   ____

Who was Deborah in the Bible?

⊙

⊙

⊙

How many times did David and Daniel pray?

⊙   ____

⊙   ____

⊙   ____

What happened when Joshua prayed?

⊙   ______________________   ⊙   ______________________

⊙   ______________________   ⊙   ______________________

MY NOTES

PRACTICING A
LIFESTYLE OF PRAYER

The word practice is defined in Webster's Dictionary as something that is frequently repeated. It is a customary action; habitual performance; a succession of acts of a similar kind; usage; habit or custom. It can include the practice of rising early; making regular entries of accounts; and daily exercise (Webster, 2021). The Collins Harper Dictionary defines lifestyle as a set of attitudes, habits, or possessions associated with a particular person or group (Harper, 2021).

Author, Jack Hayford offers three simple ways to practice and cultivate our walk with Jesus. He recommends to

- Enter God's presence by thanking Him and giving Him praise, and worship Him. Mark 12:30
- Open our hearts to God, asking forgiveness and for the cleansing of our hearts. Proverbs 4:23
- Speak blessings over our day. 1 Peter 5:6-11

To master the examples given, you will need some of the following tools:

- A Repentant Heart
- A good study Bible
- Bible dictionary
- Focus
- Journal

MARCH

DATE

MEETING GOALS

- ○
- ○
- ○

LIST THE THINGS YOU CAN DO TO BE MORE COMMITTED TO PRAYER AS A LEADER.

- ○
- ○
- ○
- ○

WORD FOR THE MONTH: COMMITMENT

WAYS YOU PLAN ON PROMOTING COMMITMENT WITH TEAM MEMBERS.

WHAT HAPPENS WHEN YOU ARE COMMITTED TO A LIFESTYLE OF PRAYER?

LIST THREE COMMITMENT PRACTICES.

HOW WOULD YOU RANK TODAY'S MEETING?

☆ ☆ ☆ ☆ ☆

A fool vents all his feelings, but a wise man holds them back."
Proverbs 29:11

Name: ________________   **Date:** ____________

14 Ways
to Practice a Lifestyle of Prayer

Put a check beside the prayer practice that you use.

- ☐ Start by Asking God for His Help
- ☐ Begin with praise and worship
- ☐ Pray God's Word
- ☐ Use visual reminders
- ☐ Be committed and consistent
- ☐ Be persistent and persevere
- ☐ Walk in obedience
- ☐ Find some prayer partners
- ☐ Be accountable
- ☐ Find a quiet place
- ☐ Decide on the time that's best for you
- ☐ Use a daily journal
- ☐ Record what God shares with you
- ☐ Read or listen to scriptures daily
- ☐ Practice listening for directions and instructions

List three ways you practice prayer in your daily life:

____

____

____

Name: _________________   **Date:** _____________

PRAYER LIFESTYLE

At times Jesus Himself had to be unplugged from the demands of a busy day. Like you and I, He needed His battery recharged so he would slip away to the wilderness to spend time with God. Even though Jesus had all power in His hands, the practice of prayer as a lifestyle was evident. Jesus prayed regularly to seek guidance from our Heavenly Father. He constantly renewed his mind, received advice, and was refreshed so He could handle all of the challenges that came before Him.

Luke 5:16 states that Jesus plugged directly into the source where His purpose, power, and provisions begin, and that was with God whenever He slipped away to pray. Jesus modeled His prayer life so well that in (Matthew 6:9-13) His disciple asked, "Lord teach us to pray." One of the best weapons given to us is the power of prayer.

Practicing a lifestyle of prayer has benefits.

1. You will recognize whom you are speaking to
2. You will begin to repent and ask for forgiveness
3. You will thank God regularly throughout the day
4. You will ask for His will in your life
5. You will begin to memorize scripture
6. Pray more for family, friends, enemies, and the world at large
7. Ask for your needs to be met
8. Ask for the needs of others to be met

List which prayer practice you are doing right now in your life.

Which prayer practice do you need to improve on?

Name: ________________   **Date:** ____________

MY FUTURE PRAYER VISION

PRAYER GOALS

⊙ ____

⊙ ____

⊙ ____

TIME & PLACE

⊙ ____

⊙ ____

⊙ ____

PERSONAL ACHIEVEMENTS

⊙ ____

⊙ ____

⊙ ____

CHARACTER STRENGTHS

⊙ ______________________   ⊙ ______________________

⊙ ______________________   ⊙ ______________________

LIFESTYLE TRACKER

Use this tool as a checklist to track your activities during the week for one month. Score yourself using 1-5, with 1 being the lowest score.

Daily Activity	S	M	T	W	T	F	S
Wake up early							
Take a shower							
Read or listen to SCRIPTURE							
Write a journal							
DRESS FOR THE DAY							
Drink Plenty of Water							
Take medication							
Eat healthy meals during the day							
Exercise							
Work on something meaningful							
Accomplish Daily Goal(s)							

MY NOTES

Team Building & Relationship

Jesus was a leader, and the focus of His leadership was empowering others to live out God's plan for their lives, not their own agendas. He served His disciples through a clear mission, direction, training, and a team of focused leaders to continue the mission of reconciliation after He returned to the Father.

When we observe Jesus' life, we see four key elements of His leadership.

- Jesus had a clear mission. Jesus was a servant to the Father's mission for His life: to be the Suffering Servant Messiah (Isa. 53:11), "to give His life—a ransom for many" (Mark 10:45). He didn't come to do His will "but the will of Him who sent Me" (John 6:38). Jesus humbled Himself and became a servant to God's mission for His life (Phil. 2:6-8). The mission of God first belonged to Jesus. The mission of God is everything for a servant leader who follows Jesus, answering the question "Why are we here?" The most familiar statement of this mission is what we call the Great Commission (Matthew 28:19-20). As followers of Jesus go about their lives, we're to "make disciples" (v. 19) of Jesus. More specifically, God has commissioned with us the "ministry of reconciliation" (2 Corinthians 5:18), in which we are "ambassadors for Christ" where we live, learn, work, and play (v. 20).
- Jesus provided a clear direction. Jesus influenced His followers to leave their status quo and go where they wouldn't go on their own. The direction Jesus provided enabled His disciples to answer the question "Where are we going?" Jesus led them to trust "the kingdom of God has come near" and to "repent and believe in the good news" of His coming (Mark 1:15). He told vision stories in the form of parables to help them see God's preferred future for them. Jesus led those who trusted Him to the cross, where He suffered and died but was raised on the third day. Jesus kept the purposes and plans of God before His followers through His actions, teachings, and stories. Servant leaders like Jesus continually tell those they lead where they're going and what their lives are becoming through a loving relationship with Jesus Christ. This is the vision of a servant leader like Jesus.
- Jesus trained His disciples to carry out the Father's mission. Jesus equipped them through His "Follow Me" method of training (Matthew 4:19) and trained them with the skills to be Kingdom people through His teaching and example. Equipping answers, to the question of those who join us on a mission, "How do we do this?"
- Jesus invested in a team of disciples. At the end of three years, when Jesus' time came to return to the Father, He commissioned His disciples to continue God's mission of reconciliation (Matthew 28:19-20). To lead as a servant leader like Jesus is to invest in a core group of leaders who will carry on the mission in the leader's absence. Team leadership answers the question "Whom can we count on?"

April

MEETING GOALS

-
-
-

LIST FOUR WAYS TO BUILD RELATIONSHIPS.

-
-
-
-

WORD FOR THE MONTH: RELATIONSHIP

WAYS YOU PLAN ON PROMOTING RELATIONSHIP BUILDING WITH TEAM MEMBERS.

WHY IS BUILDING A RELATIONSHIP WITH YOUR TEAM IMPORTANT?

LIST THREE REASONS WHY YOU NEED TO HAVE A RELATIONSHIP WITH GOD.

HOW WOULD YOU RANK TODAY'S MEETING?

☆ ☆ ☆ ☆ ☆

5 Minute Prayer Journaling

"Let nothing be done through selfish ambition or conceit, but in lowliness of mind let each esteem others better than himself. Let each of you look out not only for his own interests, but also for the interests of others."
Philippians 2:3-4

QUESTION

TIME

BUILDING RELATIONSHIPS

Being a Christian leader can be filled with loneliness. It is helpful to have a small group of trusted individuals to whom one may reveal vulnerabilities and receive Godly feedback. Jesus saw the importance of communion in the spirit in prayer for those who followed him so they would be able to receive the joy of the Lord. Christian leaders need to develop and build relationships with individuals, so they can learn and benefit from their experiences.

List the four key elements of Jesus' leadership mentioned on the team and relationship-building relationship page.

1.

2.

3.

4.

BUILDING RELATIONSHIP AS YOU

Examine Yourself

Do you follow any of these principles as a team builder? Score yourself on a scale of 1-5 with 1 being the lowest number.

1. Do you have clear goals and a Biblical purpose?
2. Do you have a method to monitor people's performance without being arrogant?
3. Do your goals include the spiritual growth of yourself and the team?
4. Do you have clear job descriptions and a line of command?
5. Do you spend time encouraging your team to spiritual growth?
6. Do you know how to lead yourself and others to bring the church more profound into the heart of God to worship and glorify Him?
7. Do your team members possess the competence, abilities, and skills to carry out these goals?
8. Do your team members have a deep reverence and love for the Lord, so it infuses them and their personality and spills out to others around them? (Keep in mind team members' different personalities and spiritual maturity.)
9. Do the ministry's goals take a back seat to service, love, and care?
10. Do you have a personal agenda that occupies your primary focus?
11. Do you have a sense of unified commitment within your team, so they feel a sharing of the ministry, or is there just one person running the show?
12. Is there a sense of love and trust within the team?
13. Do you hold regular meetings, listen, and welcome their input?
14. Does your team trust you and know that you care and listen so that they share their perceptions and give you feedback?
15. Do you encourage improvement without imposing pressure?
16. Does your team have the necessary resources, supplies, and support to complete the work?
17. Does your team feel appreciated?
18. Do you build on one another's strengths and protect and complement one another's weaknesses?
19. Do you allow your team the freedom to fail without judging or showing condescension?
20. Does your team support you and help you achieve goals, or is there competition and back fighting?
21. Do you have the ability to confront sin and take risks, setting the example for the team?
22. Do you listen to new ideas from your team?
23. Do the church and upper leadership, including the pastor(s), support you and your team?
24. Have you spent adequate time with training?
25. Are you open to improvement?
26. How much time are you and your team spending in prayer, personally and collectively?

If prayer is not occupying at least 1/3 of your meeting times, your priorities are off!

EXAMINE YOURSELF

Read each statement below, and as you examine yourself, circle the number that best describes your interaction and relationship with your ministry. Score yourself using 1 as the lowest and 5 as the highest. At the bottom of the page total your score from each column, then add the score from each column to get your total.

Score Scale
100-80 Above Average
79-59   Average
58-38 Below Average

		1	2	3	4	5
1.	As a team do you have clear goals and a Biblical purpose?	1	2	3	4	5
2.	Do your goals include the spiritual growth of yourself and the team?	1	2	3	4	5
3.	Do you have a clear description and a line of command as a team?	1	2	3	4	5
4.	Do you spend time encouraging your team to spiritual growth?	1	2	3	4	5
5.	Do you know how to lead yourself and others to bring the church more profound into the heart of God to worship and glorify Him?	1	2	3	4	5
6.	Do you believe that your team members possess the competence, abilities, and skills to carry out your ministry goals?	1	2	3	4	5
7.	Do your team members have a deep reverence and love for the Lord, so it infuses them and their personality and spills out to others around them?	1	2	3	4	5
8.	Do you use an agenda that occupies your primary focus in your meeting?	1	2	3	4	5
9.	Do you have a sense of unified commitment within your team, so they feel a sharing of the ministry, or is there just one person running the show?	1	2	3	4	5
10.	Do your ministry sense love and trust within the team?	1	2	3	4	5
11.	Does your ministry hold regular meetings, listen, and welcome input from team members?	1	2	3	4	5
12.	Does your team have the necessary resources, supplies, and support to complete the necessary task?	1	2	3	4	5
13.	Does your team feel appreciated?	1	2	3	4	5
14.	As a ministry do you build on one another's strengths and protect and complement one another's weaknesses?	1	2	3	4	5
15.	Do you allow your team the freedom to fail without judging or showing condescension?	1	2	3	4	5
16.	As a team do you support and help each other achieve goals, or is there competition and back fighting?	1	2	3	4	5
17.	Are you willing to listen to new ideas from your team?	1	2	3	4	5
18.	Are you willing to spend adequate time receiving additional training?	1	2	3	4	5
19.	Do you believe it is important to be open to improvement?	1	2	3	4	5
20.	Are you and your team spending time in prayer, personally and collectively?	1	2	3	4	5
	Total					

JESUS WAS INTENTIONAL ABOUT
TEAM AND RELATIONSHIP BUILDING

Who did Jesus build up?

- ⊙ ____
- ⊙ ____
- ⊙ ____

What occupations did some of the disciples have before they started following Jesus?

- ⊙ ____
- ⊙ ____
- ⊙ ____

How did Jesus serve His disciples?

- ⊙ ____
- ⊙ ____
- ⊙ ____

What was the focus of Jesus' leadership?

- ⊙ ____
- ⊙ ____

MY NOTES

Setting Aside Time to Spend with God

Time with God is essential. It takes discipline to establish routine communication and time in His presence.

Fun Facts:

One must learn to turn off the TV, computer, iPad, and cellphone, so he can hear the Lord as he studies the Word and worship God.

God deserves our time because He is the one who gives us time. Someone might not be an early riser, but he needs to set aside time that best fits his schedule when seeking God.

Spending Time Reminders

- Set a visual reminder (sticky notes)
- Create a prayer vision board
- Set a timer on your watch, computer, phone, or iPad

Let's Chat:

MAY

MEETING GOALS

○ ______________________________

○ ______________________________

○ ______________________________

LIST A FEW VISUAL REMINDERS FOR PRAYER.

○ ______________________________

○ ______________________________

○ ______________________________

○ ______________________________

WORD FOR THE MONTH:
TIME-MANAGEMENT

____

____

____

WAYS YOU PLAN ON PROMOTING TIME-MANAGEMENT WITH TEAM MEMBERS.

____

____

DATE

____

HOW CAN YOU ELIMINATE DISTRACTIONS WHEN SPENDING TIME WITH GOD?

____

____

____

____

____

LIST THREE OBSTACLES TO MANAGING YOUR PRAYER TIME.

____

____

____

____

HOW WOULD YOU RANK TODAY'S MEETING?

____

☆ ☆ ☆ ☆ ☆

"But select capable men from all the people—men who fear God, trustworthy men who hate dishonest gain —and appoint them as officials over thousands, hundreds, fifties, and tens."
Exodus 18:21

When we set aside that alone time
with God, we can pour our hearts
out to God.

It is Essential!

WHAT IS ESSENTIAL?

Time with God is__________. It takes discipline to establish routine communication and time in His presence.

SCRIPTURE

Luke 5:16, illustrates what prayer meant in the life of Christ.

THE SCRIPTURE STATES:

"So, He Himself often withdrew into the wilderness and prayed."

WHAT MUST YOU DO?
FILL IN THE BLANKS

One must _________ to turn off the TV, computer, iPad, and cellphone so he can hear the ________ as he studies the _________ and worship God.

Ideas ON
Spending Time with God
Incredible

"God invites everyone to a breathing, nurturing and growing relationship by spending time with Him (Graham, 2021)"

Reading His Word

Studying His Word

Memorizing His Word

Meditating on His Word

Alone time

The lifestyle of Purpose through Prayer

Name: _______________________   Date: _______________________

GOAL
SETTING

Write down one goal for each area in the spaces below. Think about what you want to achieve by the end of the year.

MEMORIZING SCRIPTURE

____

READING THE WORD

____

ALONE TIME WITH GOD

____

Dreamin'
Write your prayer goals in the bubble!

MY NOTES

TIME MANAGEMENT
THINK ABOUT A TYPICAL DAY

As a Christian Leader, it is imperative to manage your time wisely. Good time-management skills are essential for leaders. When you can use your time effectively, you can get more done and are less likely to feel overwhelmed. Leaders are constantly juggling priorities and trying to do more with less time. To successfully lead, they need to learn how to manage their time efficiently.
Following these tips will help you to be more productive and stress-free.

THINK ABOUT...

- To improve your time-management skills set goals. You are more likely to stay focused and motivated when you have specific goals.
- A to-do list is another essential tool for effective time management. When you have a list of tasks to complete, you are less likely to procrastinate or forget crucial tasks.
- Make a list of the things that you want to share. Share at least three to five different ideas and try to find ways that you can share your thoughts. Reading, talking, writing, and listening are all terrific ways for you to share your thoughts.
- As a leader, you should have some time for yourself. You must get the proper rest because your effectiveness will suffer if you do not. It would help if you carved out some time to spend with yourself.
- Put your phone away when busy. If you constantly stay connected to your phone, you will become distracted. It would help if you committed to putting your phone away and focusing on the task.
- Stop procrastinating, you are holding up productivity. Procrastination is a bad habit, and it is imperative to stop putting things off until the last minute.

JUNE

HOW CAN TIME-MANAGEMENT
HELP YOU SPEND MORE TIME WITH
GOD?

MEETING GOALS

○

○

○

LIST FOUR REASONS THAT TIME-
MANAGEMENT IS IMPORTANT.

○

○

○

○

LIST THREE REASONS WHY YOU
NEED TIME-MANAGEMENT.

WORD FOR THE MONTH: TIME-
MANAGEMENT

WAYS YOU PLAN ON PROMOTING
TIME-MANAGEMENT WITH
TEAM MEMBERS.

HOW WOULD YOU RANK TODAY'S
MEETING?

☆ ☆ ☆ ☆ ☆

5 Minute Prayer Journaling

"So, then, be careful how you live. Do not be unwise but wise, making the best use of your time because the times are evil. Therefore, do not be foolish, but understand what the Lord's will is."
Ephesians 5:15-17

6 Time Management Tips

- Set your goals

- Make a schedule (to-do-list)

- Prioritize thoughts

- Spend time on yourself

- Put your phone away

- Stop procrastination

Time Management

READ THOROUGHLY AND THEN ANSWER THE QUESTIONS.

Read the short passage below and answer each of the questions in complete sentences.

The sun glistened into my bedroom window. I could hear the birds chirping outside because I'd left my window slightly open overnight. Even though the sun was beaming, the air was cool. I snuggled down into my quilt, not ready to get out of bed just yet.

I heard a knock at my door. 'Remy - are you awake?'
It sounded like my best friend Sam. 'Come in,' I responded.

Sam slowly opened the door and peeked inside. As he moved into my room, I could see he was wearing his favourite blue denim backpack. Before I knew it, Sam had jumped onto my bed and started rambling about his adventure to Mount Champion with his dad the day before.

'Remy! Seriously - you won't believe what we found,' he started. 'We were walking along the creek and I spotted a bright green frog with an injured leg! I caught it, Remy - we've named him Bill! We're going to take him to Wildlife Rescue this afternoon.'

What happens when you procrastinate?

____

How can you eliminate distractions?

____

What boundaries do you need to set to eliminate distractions in your daily schedule?

____

What happens when you try to multitask?

____

____

Why do you need to prioritize your daily schedule?

____

Name: _________________   Date: ______________

Time-Management Activity

In the space provided, list four tasks you need help with managing your time.

↘ **TASK #1**

Due Date:

Status:

↘ **TASK #2**

Due Date:

Status:

↘ **TASK #3**

Due Date:

Status:

↘ **TASK #4**

Due Date:

Status:

Name: _________________   Date: ______________

TIME-MANAGEMENT

Use this sheet to manage your schedule. Write out your daily task.

Additional Notes

DATE

MY NOTES

PRIORITIZING YOUR TIME

Christian leaders must be intentional about how they prioritize their time as a leader. It is my belief that Christ should be our number one priority. Our next priority should be our family and then our career. Following our obligations in our church— lastly, self-improvement and maintaining a proper diet and exercise. If a Christian leader has not put Christ as his top priority, it will be difficult to accomplish any of the other essential things in his life. It takes time and experience through prayer that will help Christian leader to put their priorities in order.

Numerous strategies of prayer practices to prioritize prayer disciplines are used (Larry J. Michael, 2010). Below you will see the list he suggests. Rewrite the list of priorities used by Michael. His book is Spurgeon on Leadership: Key Insights for Christians Leaders from the Prince of Preachers. Grand Rapids: Kregel Publication.

1) ___________________________________

2) ___________________________________

3) ___________________________________

4) ___________________________________

5) ___________________________________

6) ___________________________________

7) ___________________________________

8) ___________________________________

9) ___________________________________

10) ___________________________________

11) ___________________________________

This is the list that Michael's suggest:

1) Intentional prayer discipline daily
2) Write a love letter to Jesus
3) Be authentic and honest with God
4) Bible Study
5) Use a Bible dictionary
6) Journal Notebook
7) Posture practice-Kneeling- bowing-standing, sitting
8) Reading from the book of Psalms daily
9) Praying the Scriptures
10) Use index cards for Scripture memory practice
11) Persevere in your prayer life even when it seems difficult

JULY

MEETING GOALS

- ○ _______________________
- ○ _______________________
- ○ _______________________

FOUR THINGS YOU NEED TO PRIORITIZE.

- ○ _______________________
- ○ _______________________
- ○ _______________________
- ○ _______________________

WORD FOR THE MONTH: PRIORITIZE

WAYS YOU PLAN ON PROMOTING
PRIORITIZING WITH TEAM MEMBERS.

DATE

____

HOW CAN YOU PRIORITIZE YOUR TIME
WITH GOD?

LIST THREE REASONS WHY YOU
NEED TO PRIORITIZE YOUR DAY.

HOW WOULD YOU RANK TODAY'S
MEETING?

☆ ☆ ☆ ☆ ☆

5 Minute Prayer Journaling

"And he spake a parable unto them to this end, that men ought always to pray, and not to faint."
(Luke 18:1)

PRIORITIZE YOUR DAILY PLANNER

Date_____________   ⭕ Mon   ⭕ Tue   ⭕ Wed   ⭕ Thu   ⭕ Fri

WHAT ARE YOUR TOP THREE PRIORITIES:

1 ▬▬▬▬   2 ▬▬▬▬   3 ▬▬▬▬

7 am
8 am
9 am
10 am
11 am
12 pm
1 pm
2 pm
3 pm
4 pm
5 pm
6 pm
7 pm
8 pm

MY DAILY SELF CARE

GOALS

HOW WAS YOUR DAY

30 DAYS
Priority Challenge

Use this calendar as a planner to prioritize your goals for one month.

MONTH OF:

DAY 1	DAY 2	DAY 3	DAY 4	DAY 5

DAY 6	DAY 7	DAY 8	DAY 9	DAY 10

DAY 11	DAY 12	DAY 13	DAY 14	DAY 15

DAY 16	DAY 17	DAY 18	DAY 19	DAY 20

DAY 21	DAY 22	DAY 23	DAY 24	DAY 25

DAY 26	DAY 27	DAY 28	DAY 29	DAY 30

Prioritize Your Time

DECISION MAKING

Follow the prompts below to brainstorm solutions to a decision you are facing. Choose the best solution based on your answers.

What decision are you trying to make about prioritizing your time?

	Advantages of prioritizing	Disadvantages of prioritizing	Consequences of prioritizing
Solution 1			
Solution 2			
Solution 3			

What was your final finding?

Name: ________________   Date: _____________

Prioritize Your Prayer Practice

This checklist can be used to help you to be more accountable when prioritizing your daily prayer practice.

Ways to priories your prayer practice	Complete	YES	NO
Intentional prayer discipline daily			
Write a love letter to Jesus			
Be honest and authentic with God			
Bible study			
Obtain some bible tools			
Use a bible dictionary			
Regular Prayer walking exercise			
Get a Journal Notebook			
Posture yourself by practicing-Kneeling- bowing- standing, sitting			
Study the Book of Psalm			
Pray the Scriptures			
Persevere in your prayer life even when it seems difficult or overwhelming			

MY NOTES

UNDERSTANDING THE BIBLICAL PERSPECTIVE OF LEADERSHIP

The Bible is full of biblical leadership, beginning with God being our ultimate leader. Once He created the universe, He passed the leadership baton of the earth over to humankind (Genesis1:26). God created Adam and Eve to have dominion over the earth (Genesis 1:26, 28) because they possessed a ruling capability. Notice here, God created us in His image, and we are capable of leading others whether it be our family, job, church, or community. God gave us authority over the things on earth.

Colossians 3:1-2 states, "If then you were raised with Christ, seek those things which are above, where Christ is, sitting at the right hand of God. Set your mind on things above, not on things on the earth"

There is always a better way to lead. Blanchard, Hodges, and Hendry share four essential beliefs they have found to work in their ministry: the heart, the head, the hands, and the habits (Blanchard K., 2008).
- "Leadership is a way to influence the behavior, development, and thinking of others."
- "The greatest leadership role model in the world is Jesus."
- "Jesus approached his followers from a servant leadership approach."
- "Leadership should begin in our hearts to be effective."

Mike Ayers explores five components of biblical leadership and the influence of each on a leader:
- **CHARACTER**
- **CALLING**
- **COMPETENCE**
- **COMMUNITY**
- **CHRIST**

He expresses his thoughts on the influence associated with each component:

CHARACTER: The leader, who takes on the character of Christ in an authentic way, will be able to influence those he serves.

CALLING: The call comes from God, who will use a leader to influence others to stay future-focused to achieve his plan. God called Moses to deliver the people from the bondage of slavery. He called Joshua to replace Moses to lead the people into the Promised Land, and he also called Nehemiah to rebuild the walls of Jerusalem.

COMPETENCE: A leader needs authentic character and a calling to lead with competence. Being competent will enable one to influence those he leads.

COMMUNITY: The people we lead can determine whether we have a heart for them. They will feel our love and compassion, which will help an individual to build a community.

CHRIST: A leader's real power can only come from God. As humans, this type of power is beyond our intellect. Jesus imparted the Holy Spirit to indwell biblical leaders so they could live, love, lead and serve others.

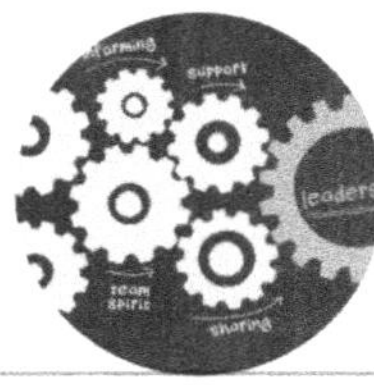

AUGUST

DATE

____

MEETING GOALS

○ ______________________________

○ ______________________________

○ ______________________________

LIST FOUR WAYS TO IMPROVE YOUR CHARACTER.

○ ______________________________

○ ______________________________

○ ______________________________

○ ______________________________

WORD FOR THE MONTH: CHARACTER

WAYS YOU PLAN ON PROMOTING GOOD CHARACTER WITH TEAM MEMBERS.

LIST THREE CHARACTER TRAITS YOU NEED TO WORK ON.

LIST YOUR BEST CHARACTER TRAITS.

HOW WOULD YOU RANK TODAY'S MEETING?

☆ ☆ ☆ ☆ ☆

5 Minute Prayer Journaling

"Take my yoke upon you and learn from me, for I am gentle and humble in heart, and you will find rest for your souls."
Matthew 11:29

Name: __________________   **Date:** _____________

THE CHRIST-LIKE CHARACTER OF A SERVANT LEADER

As Christians, we have a huge advantage of having Jesus as our leadership role model. We are called to daily grow to be more Christ-like in our lives. That includes being a leader. Jesus was the supreme servant leader. He was focused on enabling his people to grow into maturity and achieve their full potential for God's Kingdom's purposes. The challenge for us is to become Christ-Centered Servant Leaders. This is about both developing a Christ-like character and developing leadership skills that equip us to lead others in a way that is empathetic to being a Christ-centered servant leader. Below you can view some of the characteristics a servant leader should have. Circle the characteristic that best fit your leadership style.

A Servant's Heart	Even Tempered	Loving
Honesty	Joyful	Wise
Loyalty	Gentle	Discerning
Perseverance	Consistent	Encouraging
Trustworthiness	Spiritual Depth	Passionate
Courage	Forgiving	Fair
Humility	Compassionate	Patient
Sensitivity	Energetic	Kind
Teachable	Faithful	Merciful
Values Driven	Self-Controlled	Reliable
Optimistic		

LIST THE CHARACTERISTIC THAT YOU NEED TO WORK ON.

____

Take the free Spiritual Gifts Test
https://giftstest.com/test

Name: ________________   **Date:** ____________

COMPETENCE OF A SERVANT LEADER

Joshua's leadership competence was evident in his ability to lead, demonstrating his ability to get results. Joshua received on-the-job training under Moses's tutorage, which allowed him to continue developing his leadership skills. He was trusted by God to spy out the Promise Land and to accompany Moses to Mount Sinai until he was stopped halfway up the mountain. Moses mentored Joshua, and he replaced him upon his death. Joshua's opportunity to lead came from his great success as a military leader, which prepared him for a much more significant role. He served Moses for 40 years as he grew in his competence. He was unwilling to leave Moses because he wanted to learn as much as possible. Once Moses changed Joshua's name to Hoshea's, which means "salvation," his life transformed to a level of being able to delegate, organize, and lead the nation of Israel. His training from Moses paid off.

Write True or False beside each statement?

1. Joshua was Moses's mentor. ____

2. Joshua served Moses for 20 years. ____

3. Joshua's life was transformed after his name was changed. ____

4. Joshua did not have the ability to delegate or organize the people. ____

LEADERSHIP CHARACTER

Mark your answers as **True** or **False** and find a scripture that is associated with your answer.
All scriptures are listed below.

1. A leader's morality does not affect those under him/her. _____
2. All positions of power are ordained by God. _____
3. Once decided, a leader's heart cannot be changed. _____
4. A good leader does not need counselors. _____
5. Leadership that encourages good deeds, exalts a nation. _____
6. Wicked leaders cannot succeed. _____
7. A wicked leader's end is guaranteed destruction. _____
8. Joseph found favor in the eyes of his master because he was intelligent

    _____
9. Moses was a leader noted for his eloquent speech. _____
10. Moses was the humblest man on earth. _____
11. Moses took the responsibility for the Israelites' sin. _____
12. Though a great leader, Joshua needed confidence. _____
13. God did not intend for Israel to be ruled by a king. _____
14. From the beginning, Saul demonstrated cowardliness in leadership. _____
15. Social position and appearance are pivotal to success as a leader. _____
16. Before taking leadership, David demonstrated respect for his predecessor,
    even though they were enemies. _____
17. As a leader, Solomon asked God for discernment to rule rather than for
    riches. _____
18. Wisdom in leadership comes from God. _____
19. Josiah was an example of a six-year-old leader. _____
20. Leadership may entail integrity at the cost of your life. _____

Proverbs 29:12	Psalm 37:35-38	II Chronicles 9:23	Hebrew 13:17	Romans 13:1
Genesis 39:2-4	Proverbs 21:1	II Chronicles 34:1-2	Numbers 12:3	Ester 4:15-16
Matthew 7:28-29	Proverbs 15:22	Matthew 8:8-10	Proverbs 14:32	Mark 10:42-45
I Samuel 24:5-6	Exodus 32:30-32	Joshua 1:7-9	I Samuel 10:20-22	I Samuel 8:4-7

Determining the Importance of Calling

CALLING: The call comes from God, who will use a leader to influence others to stay future-focused to achieve his plan. God called Moses to deliver the people from the bondage of slavery. He called Joshua to replace Moses to lead the people into the Promised Land, and he also called Nehemiah to rebuild the walls of Jerusalem.

Answer the following questions.

1. Where does a person's call come from?

2. What did God call Moses to do?

3. What did God call Nehemiah to do?

4. What did God call Joshua to do?

Important facts about calling:
What do you believe God has called you to do?

MY NOTES

Now ask yourself:

1. How do I exhibit Servant Leadership in my daily life?
2. What can I do to develop a better willingness to have a serving attitude in leadership and value people rather than manipulate them?
3. What blocks Servant Leadership from working and being exhibited in me?
4. How can I make Servant Leadership function better, stronger, and faster, even in times of uncertainty and stress?

WHAT IS LEADERSHIP

Leadership is defined as influencing and serving others. As we look at Matthew 20:25-28, it teaches us that we lead by serving and serve by leading. "Anyone wanting to be a leader among you must be your servant." Our attitudes need to be like Jesus; He was a servant first. Luke 22:26 states "But among you, the one who serves best will be your leader." Our role as a leader includes helping others as we serve. Jesus demonstrated His leadership when He regularly went away to a solitary place to get directions and guidance from His Father before the start of the day.

SOME CHARACTERISTICS OF A SERVANT LEADER

- They must not serve two masters. (Matt. 6:24)
- They must be last. (Mark 9:35)
- They must humble themselves. (Mark 10:3-45)
- They must sacrifice themselves. (Luke 3:10-11)
- Can be recognized by their actions. (Luke 3:30-37)
- They must be seeking eternal over temporary. (Luke 12:33-34)
- They must be examples to others. (Luke 22:27)
- They must not allow pride to dominate their life. (John 13:4-17)
- They must value and appreciate others. (John 15:12)

TEN CHARACTERISTICS AS DEFINED BY SPEARS INCLUDE:

1. Lends a listening and understanding ear.
2. Shows empathy to those in need.
3. Heal self and others mentally, physically and spiritual
4. Be aware of your strengths and weaknesses.
5. Be persuasive.
6. Dream Big Conceptualization.
7. Foresight the ability to see future outcomes.
8. Be a good steward.
9. Be willing to continue to grow self and others.
10. Build community

SEPTEMBER

DATE

____

MEETING GOALS

- ○ _______________________
- ○ _______________________
- ○ _______________________

LIST 4 BENEFITS OF A VISION STATEMENT.

- ○ _______________________
- ○ _______________________
- ○ _______________________
- ○ _______________________

WORD FOR THE MONTH: VISION AND PURPOSE

WAYS YOU PLAN ON PROMOTING INITIATIVE WITH TEAM MEMBERS.

WHAT DOES THE BIBLE SAY ABOUT PURPOSE?

WHAT DOES A VISION STATEMENT LOOK LIKE?

HOW WOULD YOU RANK TODAY'S MEETING?

☆ ☆ ☆ ☆ ☆

"You call me Teacher and Lord, and you are right, for so I am. If I then, your Lord and Teacher, have washed your feet, you also ought to wash one another's feet. For I have given you an example, that you also should do just as I have done to you. Truly, truly, I say to you, a servant is not greater than his master, nor is a messenger greater than the one who sent him. If you know these things, blessed are you if you do them."
John 13:13–17

Vision & Purpose

According to Jeremiah 1:5-12, the Lord said, "Before I formed you in the womb, I knew you; Before you were born, I sanctified you; I ordained you a prophet to the nations." (NIV) God was telling Jeremiah that he had a specific assignment. Jeremiah, like many others, has given all kinds of excuses as to why he could not or should not do what God was asking him to do. Then Jeremiah said, "Ah, Lord God! Behold, I cannot speak, for I am a youth." Our great and mighty God assured him that he would be given v. 7, instruction v. 8, provision v. 9, and promise v.12.

What is Vision?

The Merriam-Webster dictionary defines vision as something you imagine, a picture or dream you see in your mind (Merriam-Webster, 2022). The Hebrew word for vision is "Hazon." It is beyond the ability to see with our eyes. Hazon (H2377) is a vision that comes from God, which He and His Word reveals. Godly vision is centered around glorifying God, helping other people; it is future-focused, and it advances the Kingdom of God.

What a Vision Statement Looks Like

1. What are our hopes and dreams?
2. What problem are we solving for the greater good?
3. Who and what are we inspiring to change?

The Benefits of Having a Vision Statement

- It empowers people and focuses their efforts
- It focuses energy for greater effectiveness
- It raises the standard of excellence
- It establishes meaning for today
- It gives hope for the future
- It brings unity to the community
- It provides a sense of stability
- It raises the commitment level
- It brings positive change

Leaders can make a difference

WHAT DOES THE SCRIPTURE SAY ABOUT VISION?

Several Scriptures are reminders to seek God when in doubt about a dream or vision. Just because a leader has an idea does not mean that that idea came from God. One must ask themselves if the thoughts one received came from God. That is why Christian leaders must "not believe every spirit but test the spirit to see whether they are from God, for many false prophets have gone out into the world (1 John 4:1)." Seemingly, "Habakkuk 2:2 tells us, "And the Lord answered me: "Write the vision; make it plain on tablets, so he may run who reads it. Then Joel 2:28 echoes and says, "And it shall come to pass afterward, that I will pour out my Spirit on all flesh; your sons and your daughters shall prophesy, your old men shall dream dreams, and your young men shall see visions.

WHAT HAPPENS WHEN YOU DO PURSUE YOUR VISION?

———

ASPIRATIONS AND GOALS

YOUR FUTURE LOOKS BRIGHTER

PASSION/CREATIVITY

CLEAR DIRECTION

EFFECTIVE

WHAT HAPPENS WHEN YOU DO NOT PURSUE YOUR VISION?

———

UNFULFILLMENT

LACK OF MOTIVATION

LACK OF EXCITEMENT

NO PLAN

FEELINGS OF FRUSTRATION

TEAMWORK MAKES THE DREAM WORK

VISION BOARD

WRITE ONE GOAL FOR EACH LIFESTYLE SHOWN

FAMILY GOAL

CAREER GOAL

COMMUNITY GOAL

HEALTH GOAL

FINANCIAL GOAL

SPIRITUAL/ MINISTRY GOAL

PERSONAL GROWTH GOAL

Name: ________________   **Date:** ____________

PURPOSE

Worksheet

The word purpose has numerous meanings. The Merriam-Webster dictionary defines purpose as to why something is done or used and the aim, goal, or intention of something (Merriam-Webster, 2022). The Vine's Expository Dictionary defines purpose as "setting forth," "a purpose," used for God (Dictionary, 2022). Romans 8:28 says, "And we know that all things work together for good to those who love God, to those who are called according to His purpose."

Purpose originated from the foundation and the beginning of creation. God already had a plan and purpose for every human on earth. Our purpose was to bring glory to God. He has purposed humanity to be intelligent creatures, with gifts and talent to glorify Him and edify others. Ephesians 1:11-12 states, "In Him also we have obtained an inheritance, being predestined according to the purpose of Him who works all things according to the counsel of His will, that we who first trusted in Christ should be to the praise of His glory." Many Scriptures reveal God's purpose for our lives.

	WHO AM I	WHOM DO I BELONG TO	WHY DO I EXIST
SOLUTION 1			
SOLUTION 2			
SOLUTION 3			

WHAT ARE YOUR DREAMS AND HOPES FOR YOUR MINISTRY?

____

____

____

★

MY NOTES

Name: _________________   Date: _____________

LEADERSHIP *Qualities*

Use the next page to list the top 5 qualities you believe are important for all leaders to have:

1
2
3
4
5

Think of a leader you admire. What quality about him/her are you attracted to?

Leader:

Quality:

How they demonstrated it:

Think about a leader you don't admire, and identify the quality you don't like:

Leader:

Quality:

How they demonstrated it:

OCTOBER

DATE

MEETING GOALS

FOUR THINGS YOU NEED TO BE MORE SELF-DISCIPLINED ON.

WORD FOR THE MONTH:
SELF-DISCIPLINE

WAYS YOU CAN PROMOTE SELF-DISCIPLINE WITH TEAM MEMBERS.

HOW CAN YOU BE MORE SELF-DISCIPLINED WHEN IT COMES TO SPENDING MORE TIME WITH GOD?

LIST THREE REASONS WHY YOU NEED TO BE MORE SELF-DISCIPLINED.

HOW WOULD YOU RANK TODAY'S MEETING?

☆ ☆ ☆ ☆ ☆

"Therefore an overseer must be above reproach, the husband of one wife, sober-minded, self-controlled, respectable, hospitable, able to teach,"
1 Timothy 3:2

Empathy
Integrity
Effective Communication
Resilience
Humility
Positivity
List of
LEADERSHIP
Qualities
Delegation
Vision
Confidence
Accountability
Open-minded

HOW TO USE YOUR VISION BOARD FOR LIFE-CHANGING MANIFESTATION

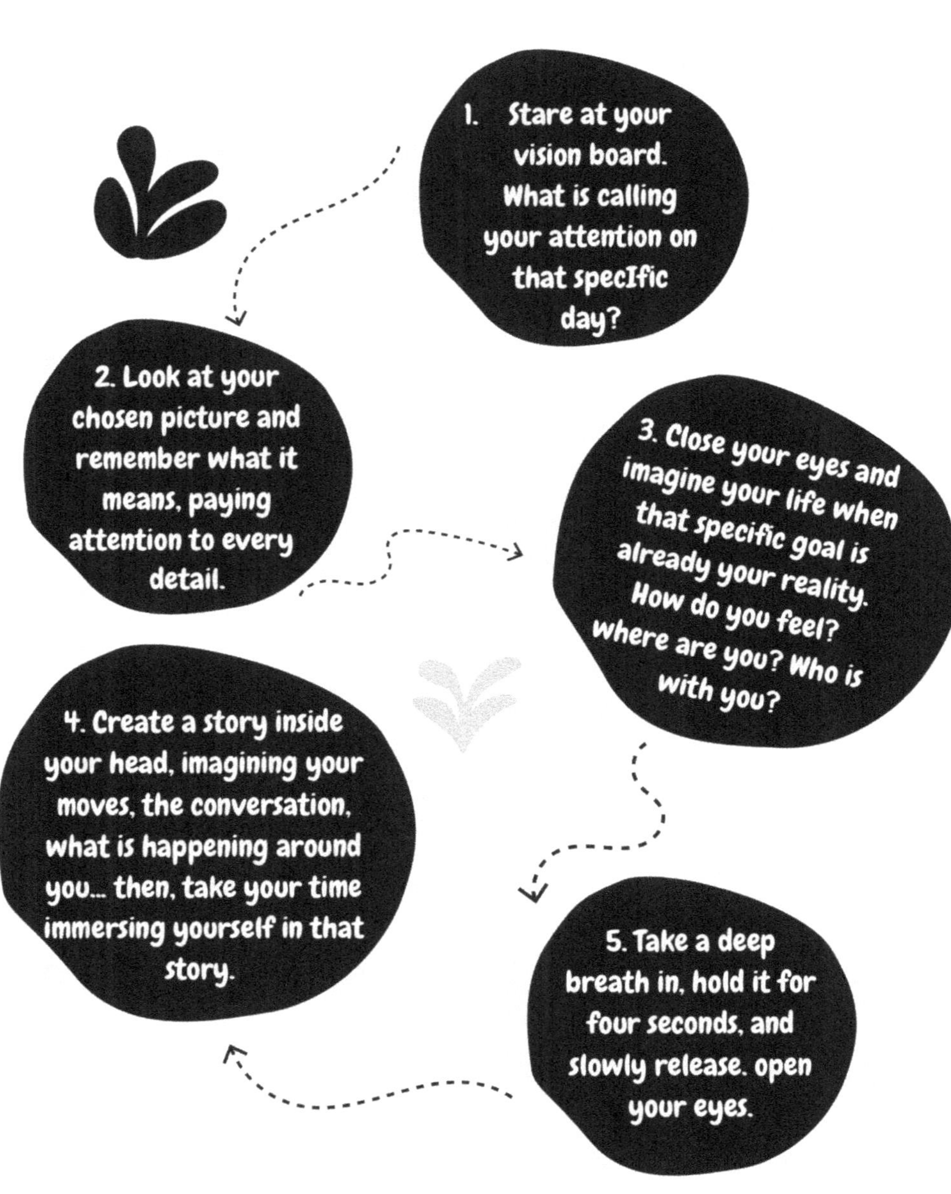

CHRISTIAN LEADERS POSSESS
THREE DISTINCT QUALITIES

FIRST, God calls a Christian leader.

SECOND, a Christian leader possesses Christ-like character.

THIRD, a Christian leader possesses functional competencies that allow him/her to perform tasks and guide people to use their abilities toward accomplishing the vision: by inspiring them, directing their energy and resources, casting vision, building teams, celebrating victories, delegating authority, making decisions, developing strategy, accepting responsibility for outcomes and so on.

THOSE WHOM GOD HAS CHOSEN TO BE
LEADERS POSSESS ALL OF THE FOLLOWING EIGHT
TRAITS:

1. DISCERNING THE CALL
2. ABSOLUTE INCLINATION
3. HAVE THE MINDSET OF A LEADER
4. NOTICEABLE INFLUENCE
5. CAPITALIZE WITHIN THE COMPANY OF LEADERS
6. EXTERNAL ENCOURAGEMENT
7. INTERNAL STRENGTH
8. LOVING IT

WHOM DOES GOD CALL TO BE A LEADER?

- First, God looks at a person's character
- Second, God can use people with or without natural ability and proper background.
- Third, God prepares those he calls.
- Fourth, God equips those he calls.

Leadership Skills

INTEGRITY

CREATIVITY

RELIABILITY

PLANNING

EMPATHY

DELEGATION

WHICH LEADERSHIP SKILL DO YOU POSSESS?

Copy the link below in your browser to take the free
Personality Test
https://www.16personalities.com/free-personality-test

MY NOTES

LEADERSHIP STYLES

Types of Leadership Styles

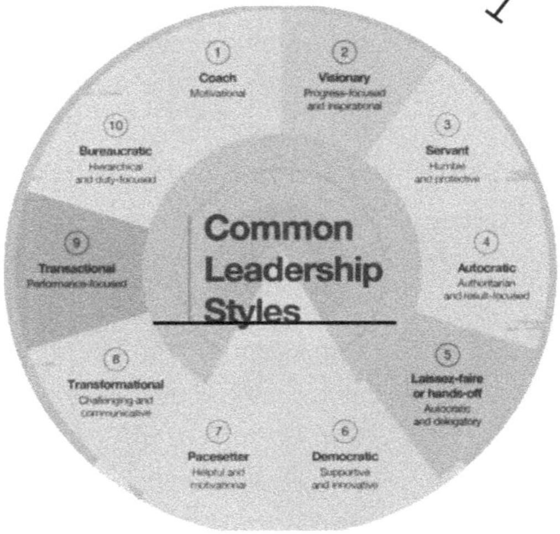

DESCRIPTIONS OF COMMONLY USED LEADERSHIP STYLES AS SHOWN IN THE CIRCLE ABOVE

Autocratic (result-focused)	**Pacesetter** (helpful and motivational)
Bureaucratic (duty- focused)	**Servant** (humble and protective)
Coach (motivational)	**Visionary** (future-focused and inspirational)
Democratic (supportive and innovative)	**Transactional** (performance focused)
Laissez-faire (hands off-delegatory)	**Transformational** (communication and challenging)

NOVEMBER

DATE
____

MEETING GOALS

○ _______________________

○ _______________________

○ _______________________

WHICH LEADERSHIP STYLE FITS
YOU THE BEST?

○ _______________________

○ _______________________

○ _______________________

○ _______________________

WORD FOR THE MONTH:
LEADERSHIP STYLE

WAYS YOU PLAN ON PROMOTING
TEACHABILITY WITH TEAM
MEMBERS.

DESCRIBE A SERVANT

LIST THREE LEADERSHIP STYLES.

HOW WOULD YOU RANK
TODAY'S MEETING?

☆ ☆ ☆ ☆ ☆

"Be diligent to present yourself approved to God, a worker who does not need to be ashamed, rightly dividing the word of truth. But shun profane and idle babblings, for they will increase to more ungodliness."
2 Timothy 2:15-16

LEADERSHIP STYLES

Looking at the several types of leadership styles can be a useful tool for Christian leaders. This Journal will explain and show the various types of leadership styles not to discredit any of them. It is designed to merely equip leaders to know the difference and to identify which category they fit in.

The Autocratic Leadership Style is when a leader decides what goals are to be achieved and directs all activities without any meaningful participation from the team. Democratic Leadership Style is when a leader allows members of the team to take a more involved role in the decision-making process. A Laissez-faire Leadership Style is when a leader is hands-off and allows team members to make decisions. The Democratic Style of Leadership tends to be an effective style because it is two-way open communication instead of one person controlling all the decisions. Looking at all the various styles of leadership and communication styles explained:

Which category do you fit in?

____

Which leadership style describes you?

____

Characteristic and Leadership Styles

LEADER TYPES	CHARACTERISTIC STYLE	LEADERS WHO POSSESS LEADERSHIP STYLES
AUTOCRATIC	Controlling, lacks flexibility, lack of listening skills, knows when to be strict and makes all plans.	Helen Gurley Brown, known for getting things done. Her autocratic style turned into profit for more than three decades in publishing.
BUREAUCRATIC	Strict, controlling, others' opinions do not matter, can be defiant, detail-oriented, and meticulous.	Winston Churchill was known as a bureaucratic leader who used strict managing skills to make decisions. Churchill took the English language to another level by being defiant and lightly humorous. He was persistent in fulfilling his plans.
CHARISMATIC	Self-confident, passionate, celebrate, or correct with a handwritten note, and helps others.	Jack Welch, the youngest CEO in General Electric, developed a positive and personal relationship with those he worked alongside. He possessed a charismatic leadership style.
COACHING	Supportive, guides vs. command, prepare for the future, identify strengths and weaknesses, motivates, trains, and improves performance.	Bill Walsh, the San Francisco 49ers head coach, led a losing team into 5 Super Bowl championships. His focus was on training, developing, and coaching to improve overall results in his players.
DEMOCRATIC	Uses a team approach, creative, group feedback, listens to others' opinions, and participative leadership style.	Dr. William Mayo and his son founded the Mayo Clinic. They are known for their democratic leadership style. They were about creating a collaborative environment where people's ideas and opinions were listened to and combined with different levels of knowledge to get the results they needed.
LAISSEZ-FAIRE	Not directly involved, trusting, gives ongoing feedback, does not micro-manage, abreast of what's going on.	Donna Karan, the founder of the DKNY Jeans Company, is known for being hands-off yet attentive, keeping her eyes on her company's profits. She trusted her managers to make wise decisions as she monitored their performance and gave feedback as needed.
PACESETTER	Sets high standards, is performance-driven, requires accountability, requires quick results .expects competence	Jack Welch was known for being a charismatic and pacesetter style of leadership. He did things in excellence, was self-directed, worked with competent teams, and made personal contact.
SERVANT	Team player, open to new ideas, one-on-one listener, encourages team, believes in the strengths of others.	Cheryl Bachelder, the founder CEO of Popeyes Louisiana Kitchen, exhibited servant leadership during her tenure. She felt that serving others was a powerful way of helping others. Her book is entitled "Dare to Serve" because of her beliefs about being a servant leader.
TRANSFORMATIONAL	Sees the big picture, mindset changeable, charismatic, influencer, a goal setter, team player.	Lee Iacocca, chairman of the Chrysler Corporation on the brink of bankruptcy, transformed it into a profitable business. Today he is called the father of the Ford Mustang. Wrote a book called "Where Have All the Leaders Gone?"
VISIONARY	Focus on the big picture; future focus, stresses innovative thinking, promotes unity, striving toward the finish line.	Sara Blakely, founder, and CEO of Spanx took a $5,000 risk with her life savings to pursue her vision, resulting in her now Empire, Spanx.

After reviewing the information on the characteristics of a leader which characteristic best fits your personality described above.

MY NOTES

Name: _________________   **Date:** ____________

SERVANT LEADERSHIP

First of all, who is a leader? Guess what, you…. and me.

Here are some examples of leaders that I found to be good leaders. Oprah Winfrey says, "I always knew I was destined for greatness and Steve Jobs said, "Don't let the voice of others drown out your inner voice." Now think about this for a moment; are all leaders good leaders, of course not? Just look around, and I am sure you can identify some of them. Ask yourself this question, "DO I want to become a good leader? Are you ready to find out how to become a good leader? Becoming a servant leader is the best way to develop into a good leader. The best servant leader I know is Jesus Christ, according to Matthew 20:26-28 (ESV), "It shall not be so among you. But whoever would be great among you must be your servant, and whoever would be first among you must be your slave, even as the Son of Man came not to be served but to serve, and to give his life as a ransom for many."

JESUS'S BIBLICAL LEADERSHIP DEMONSTRATES HOW

- He was a servant first.
- He had self-awareness.
- He always did the will of the Father.
- He always sought to glorify the Father.
- He did NOT seek recognition for Himself.
- He was a praying leader.
- He was a gentle teacher.
- He was a preacher.
- He cared about the physical needs of His people and He still does.

SERVE OTHERS AS A SERVANT

DECEMBER

DATE

____

MEETING GOALS

○ _______________________

○ _______________________

○ _______________________

FOUR THINGS YOU NEED TO KNOW
ABOUT SERVANT LEADERS.

○ _______________________

○ _______________________

○ _______________________

○ _______________________

WORD FOR THE MONTH: SERVANT
LEADER

WAYS YOU PLAN ON PROMOTING
PRIORITIZING WITH TEAM MEMBERS.

HOW CAN YOU PRIORITIZE YOUR
TIME WITH GOD?

LIST THREE REASONS WHY YOU
NEED TO LEARN THE IMPORTANCE
OF A SERVANT LEADER.

HOW WOULD YOU RANK TODAY'S
MEETING?

☆ ☆ ☆ ☆ ☆

5 Minute Prayer Journaling

"So he shepherded them according to the integrity of his heart, And guided them with his skillful hands."

Psalms 78:72

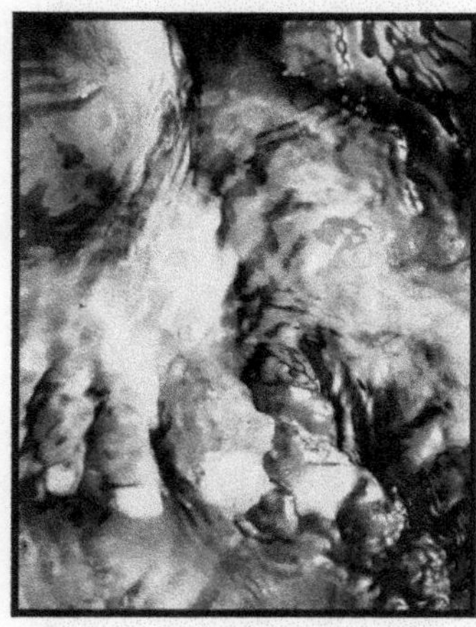

There are other leaders such as Mahatma Gandhi who stated, "We must be the change we want to see", and Martin Luther King said, "A man can't ride your back unless it is bent."

Now let's take a look again at what a servant leader looks like.

They must be:

1. A servant first.
2. Puts the needs, interests, and aspirations of others above their own.
3. Involves others in the decision-making process.
4. Enhances the personal growth of others.

JESUS, THE MODEL SERVANT LEADER

- ·Jesus **SUBMITTED** his own life to sacrificial service under the will of God: Luke 22:42 "Saying, Father, if thou be willing, remove this cup from me: nevertheless not my will, but thine, be done."
- He **SACRIFICED** his life freely out of service for others: John 10:18 "No man taketh it from me, but I lay it down of myself."
- He came to **SERVE**: Matthew 20:28 "Even as the Son of man came not to be ministered unto, but to minister, and to give his life a ransom for many."

List the three things Jesus did freely.

____

____

____

Name: _________________   Date: _____________

BIBLICAL EXAMPLES OF LEADERS

GENESIS Abraham was a friend of God
1. Abraham's leadership consisted of having faith in God.
2. He had vision, courage, and confidence.
3. Abraham stuck his neck out on behalf of others.
4. He cared about people and had a love for humanity.
5. He bargained with God to save lives.
6. He was willing to pay the ultimate price by doing what God instructed him to do.
7. He was humble.
8. He had charisma.

EXODUS Moses was one of the greatest leaders
1. Moses was goal-oriented (from slavery in Egypt to freedom in the Promised Land).
2. He cast a vision that the people were able to embrace (freedom was the key to motivating them to accomplish this).
3. He explains and showed by example the results of being obedient to God.
4. He gave his followers responsibility.
5. Moses found a way for the team to win the victory.
6. He was able to deal with internal and external conflicts.
7. Moses prepared a younger leader to take his place.
8. Moses was the meekest man on earth.

True or False
1.. Moses did not give his followers any responsibilities. _______
2. Moses was a weak man. _______
3. Abraham cared about the people and had a love for humility. ______
4. Abraham had no vision, courage, or confidence. ______
5. Moses prepared a younger leader to take his place. _______

Name: _________________   **Date:** _____________

BIBLICAL EXAMPLES OF LEADERS

JOSHUA was spiritual

As a leader, you must be spiritual

1. Joshua was in constant contact with God.
2. As a result of that, God exalted Joshua in the sight of all of Israel.
3. You must be in contact with God on a daily basis.
4. In order to be spiritual, it should be your lifestyle.
5. Joshua was willing to follow.
6. He had a vision of hope and promise.
7. He had people that were willing to follow him.
8. He challenged those around him.
9. He encouraged his followers to check things out for themselves.
10. He did not have a problem expressing himself.

DEUTERONOMY 31 (Moses and Joshua)
1. Joshua was willing to step up to the plate.
2. Good leaders learn to accept with gratitude the accomplishment of previous leaders.
3. Joshua was not envious of the great deeds of Moses.

Answer the following questions:

- What two things were Joshua willing to do?

- What was Joshua's vision?

- Was Joshua envious of the deeds of Moses?

Name: _________________   Date: _____________

Jeremiah

JEREMIAH 1 tells us that Jeremiah was a prophet God called to announce judgment on God's people because of their sin and disobedience. Jeremiah is often called the "weeping prophet" (Jer. 9:1; 13:17). For more than 40 years Jeremiah faithfully proclaimed God's judgment. Jeremiah was truly a great leader even though he was not appreciated in his leadership role.

1. God has called leaders before they were even born.
2. God usually calls younger people to be a leader.
3. God will equip those that he calls to lead.
4. Leaders who respond positively to God's will result in peace, unity, forgiveness, deliverance, healing, and abundant life.

Answer the following questions.

1. What did God call Jeremiah to do?

2. How many years did Jeremiah proclaim God's judgment?

3. What was Jeremiah often called?

4. What has God called you to do?

Weekly Planner

Monday	
Tuesday	
Wednesday	
Thursday	
Friday	
Saturday	

Reminder

Goals

Notes

MY NOTES

GAME TIME
TeamBuilding

Purpose: Team Building Activity
Time required: 20 min
Participants: Several small groups (Count off by five this will create the groups)
Purpose: To engage practical thinking
Materials needed: List of 15 people in a yacht

Instructions:

1. Each team will be given a list of 15 people who are on a yacht.
2. Scenario: The yacht developed a leak and is sinking fast.
3. There is only one lifeboat and it will accommodate only nine people not one more can fit and there are no more life boats or life jackets.
4. As a group you must come to an agreement as to which of the nine people get to go in the lifeboat to be saved.
5. You must also list those who will be saved in the order of importance, because if they run out of food and water the "less important people' will have to be dumped overboard.
6. Of course, this is often the more difficult job.
7. You will have (10 mins.) to work out the problem
8. The discussion afterward should be in depth and include everyone on the team.
   - What problems did you experience?
   - How did you resolve these issues?
   - Why did these problems occur in the first place?
   - How does this exercise reflect your day-to-day relationships?
   - What are the similarities between what you just experienced and negotiations at work and at home?

List three things you would do differently now that they have had this discussion.
Desired outcome:
   - The critical takeaway here is that cooperation often fails because each participant wants to get his or her way.
   - A better method may be to first learn the needs and intents of others.
   - Understanding fosters a spirit of cooperation and therefore agreement.

This is a list of the 15 people on the yacht THAT YOUR TEAM WILL BE DISCUSSING.
You will need to retype this list to pass it out to the groups that will be participating in this activity.

Pastor	Minister	Evangelist
A pregnant woman	A democrat	A republican
An ex-convict	A male physician	A female physician
A little boy	One African American	One white
One Hispanic	One Chinese	One Russian

FAITHFULNESS CHALLENGE

Circle the number that best describes your level of faith. Then add each row to get your final total. The number 10 is the highest-ranking number.

A Faithfulness Self Examination

F	Follow through	1	2	3	4	5	6	7	8	9	10	
A	Allegiance	1	2	3	4	5	6	7	8	9	10	
I	Integrity	1	2	3	4	5	6	7	8	9	10	
T	Trustworthy	1	2	3	4	5	6	7	8	9	10	
H	Heart	1	2	3	4	5	6	7	8	9	10	
F	Focus	1	2	3	4	5	6	7	8	9	10	
U	Unshakeable	1	2	3	4	5	6	7	8	9	10	
L	Loyalty	1	2	3	4	5	6	7	8	9	10	
N	Noble	1	2	3	4	5	6	7	8	9	10	
E	Endurance	1	2	3	4	5	6	7	8	9	10	
S	Steadfast	1	2	3	4	5	6	7	8	9	10	
S	Sacrifice	1	2	3	4	5	6	7	8	9	10	Grand Total
	Total											

Score	Comment
1–40	Low Faithfulness Motivation
41–80	Uncertainty about your Faithfulness Motivation
81–120	Strong Faithfulness Motivation

Low Faithfulness Motivation

There are several factors you need to explore to increase your level of faith.

Uncertainty about Your Faithfulness Motivation

Your faith might be going through a difficult patch, or you may want to be faithful but doubt your ability and self-confidence. You might need a nudge in the right direction.

Strong Faithfulness Motivation

If you have found that you are strongly motivated in your faithfulness, you are already in a great position to continue to move to even greater faith.

Meeting Ice Breakers

Time required: 10-15 minutes
Participants: Small groups (at least 7 in the group)
Purpose: Energizer; this game will stimulate the participants' minds and challenge their memory
Materials: Index Cards

Instructions
1. Arrange participants into two equal lines facing each other.
2. One group turns around while the other gets 30 seconds to change 10 things about them (switch jewelry, change hairstyle, untie shoelaces, switch your watch to another arm, trade clothing, etc.) as long as they are all things in sight. The first group turns back around and must identify the 10 changes.
3. After 30 seconds the second group will identify the changes that the first group made. Then they will swap so that the other team gets a chance to make changes while the other group guesses.
4. Have each group list the 10 things each group changed about themselves on an index card.

Time required: 10-15 minutes
Participants: Small groups (at least 5 in each group)
Purpose: Encourage fellow leaders in the ministry
Materials: Index Cards
Assignment: Each table will create letters addressing leadership.

Instructions
Each group will draw its question from a box. There will only be 4 questions in the box to pick from. Once they finish answering their question, they will stand before the group and discuss their answer. Must pick a leader within the group to give the response to the question.
1. Write a letter of encouragement to other leaders.
2. What does it mean to you to be a leader at your specific church?
3. What are some of the challenges of being a leader?
4. What are some of the joyful moments you have had as a leader at your church?

Time required: 10-15 minutes
Participants: Small groups of at least 6
Purpose:
Materials: Bible, Index Cards, paper, pencil, a list with the Word or Phase seen in the chart below.

Be a positive role model	Be humble	Practice effective communication
Find a mentor	Be emotionally aware	Encourage creativity
Be passionate about your work	Know your team	Think positive
Be yourself	Study	Challenge your teammates

Group Activity

Time required: 20 min
Participants: Several small groups (Count off by three-six people)
Purpose: Critical thinking
Materials needed: paper and pencil

Assignment: As a group, comes up with an ACRONYM for the word "LEADERSHIP." Then describe at least three ways that you can take our leadership responsibilities to another level.

Instruction
Place an adjective in each blank to represent each letter.

L   __________
E   __________
A   __________
D   __________
E   __________
R   __________
S   __________
H   __________
I   __________
P   __________

Discuss which Acronym was most favorable.

Leadership Quiz

Mark your answers as true or false and find a scripture that is associated with your answer. All scriptures are listed below.

1. A leader's morality does not affect those under him/her. _____
2. All positions of power are ordained by God. _____
3. Once decided, a leader's heart cannot be changed. _____
4. A good leader does not need counselors. _____
5. Leadership that encourages good deeds, exalts a nation. _____
6. Wicked leaders cannot succeed. _____
7. A wicked leader's end is guaranteed destruction. _____
8. Joseph found favor in the eyes of his master because he was intelligent. _____
9. Moses was a leader noted for his eloquent speech. _____
10. Moses was the humblest man on earth. _____
11. Moses took the responsibility for the Israelites' sin. _____
12. Though a great leader, Joshua needed confidence. _____
13. God did not intend for Israel to be ruled by a king. _____
14. From the beginning, Saul demonstrated cowardliness in leadership. _____
15. Social position and appearance are pivotal to success as a leader. _____
16. Before taking leadership, David demonstrated respect for his predecessor, even though they were enemies. _____
17. As a leader, Solomon asked God for discernment to rule rather than for riches. _____
18. Wisdom in leadership comes from God. _____
19. Josiah was an example of a six-year-old leader. _____
20. Leadership may entail integrity at the cost of your life. _____
21. People were amazed at Jesus' teaching because of its insight. _____
22. Though a leader over many, the centurion who encountered Jesus demonstrated humility _____
23. Great leadership requires a passion to be first. _____
24. Effective leadership leads through the spoken word. _____
25. Leadership responsibilities are lightened by the obedience of those under them. _____

John 13:13-17	I Samuel 16:6-7	Exodus 4:10-11	Psalm 34:35	I Kings 3:11-13
Proverbs 29:12	Psalm 37:35-38	II Chronicles 9:23	Hebrew 13:17	Romans 13:1
Genesis 39:2-4	Proverbs 21:1	II Chronicles 34:1-2	Numbers 12:3	Ester 4:15-16
Matthew 7:28-29	Proverbs 15:22	Matthew 8:8-10	Proverbs 14:32	Mark 10:42-45
I Samuel 24:5-6	Exodus 32:30-32	Joshua 1:7-9	I Samuel 10:20-22	I Samuel 8:4-7

Yearly Planner

"Write your motivational quote, here!"

January	February	March
April	May	June
July	August	September
October	November	December

Target:

Resource Page

This Leadership Workbook will support leaders who rely on prayer as their source to lead others effectively.

Available For

Speaking Engagements
Leadership Training
Coaching
Consulting
Course Creation
Workshop Facilitator

Contact Information

"Let us not become weary in doing good, for at the proper time we will reap a harvest if we do not give up."
Galatians 6:9

"Humble yourselves before the Lord, and he will lift you up."
James 4:10

"Do nothing out of selfish ambition or vain conceit. Rather, in humility value others above yourselves."
Philippians 2:3

ABOUT THE AUTHOR

Valarie is a wife, mother, grandmother, great-grandmother, teacher, preacher, psalmist, author, speaker, certified Christian Life Coach, and leadership consultant. Her greatest desire is to seek God's face and see others in the Body of Christ grow into an intimate relationship with the living Savior. Her purpose is to glorify God in everything she does. Valarie is a retired teacher who has devoted 45 years of her life to youth in the public school system. Now she serves as the Director of Ministries at Mount Olivet Baptist Church, Petersburg, VA., where she is an Associate Minister under the leadership of the Senior Pastor, Rev. Dr. Wesley K. McLaughlin. She is the owner and CEO of Stepping Out With Purpose, LLC. Valarie is the author of "Talk Time with God," "Unleashed Power of Prayer Teens and Young Adults' Prayer Journal Workbook," and the co-author of a book called "PEARLS," "Stepping Up and Stepping Out Journal Experience" and "The Effects of Prayer in the Life of a Leader Workbook."

GIVE GOD
THANKS IN
EVERYTHING

www.ingramcontent.com/pod-product-compliance
Lightning Source LLC
Chambersburg PA
CBHW040146110726
48005CB00018B/2670